Poetry &
Pigeons

Short Essays on Writing

George Franklin

Sheila-Na-Gig Editions

Poetry & Pigeons: Short Essays on Writing © 2025 George Franklin

Cover art: Peter Paillou, *Pigeon* (English, before 1790)

ISBN: 978-1-962405-14-0
Library of Congress Control Number: 2025931275

Sheila-Na-Gig Editions
Russell, KY
Hayley Mitchell Haugen, Editor
www.sheilanagigblog.com

ALL RIGHTS RESERVED
Printed in the United States of America

Acknowledgments

Most of the essays in this book were first published as blog pieces on my website: https://gsfranklin.com/. I am grateful to the following journals who either also published them in slightly different form or published them originally:

MacQueen's Quinterly: "Ten Things I Learned as a Guest Editor"

Verse Virtual: "What is a poem?"

Contents

Poetry and Pigeons	7
Why Poetry?	11
How to Write a Love Poem	13
Myths of the Poetry Biz	19
Writing About What's No Longer Here	29
Poetry and the Image	33
Translation and the Poetic	37
Prose Poems	43
The Impulse to Publish	47
Saving Poetry?	51
Defending Love & Nature	55
Ten Things I Learned as a Guest Editor	59
On the Irrational	63
Against Prompts	67
Born Too Late?	71
What Is a Poem?	77

POETRY & PIGEONS

There are days when I, like all poets and all humans, realize I should stop, look around, and ask where I am and what I'm doing here. Why am I writing poems, these undefinable creatures that refuse to do what they're told and never give us the answers we expect? Today is that kind of day. I am sitting in a square in Madrid, a square where at some long-ago time vendors sold paper, where poets and publishers might have come to purchase the raw materials of their craft. There are lots of café tables, and everyone is drinking one form of *cerveza* or another. The pigeons that gather nearby must be hungry. They're getting aggressive and even land on the tables.

What does this have to do with poetry? I suppose, I want a poem to land on my table like one of these pigeons. I want it to demand that I write it down, the way these pigeons demand bread or potato chips. Of course, that doesn't often happen, and it's definitely not happening today. So, I find myself reading the manuscript of a new book and asking myself why I've written it. The answer is complicated. Some of the poems were written out of surprise that the world exists at all, that there is something rather than nothing, surprise that the pigeon's feathers capture the sheen of sunlight and that the sky is so deeply blue. Some were written out of terror that before too long the world will still be here but the "I" of these poems will not. I'm not foolish enough to believe that poets themselves continue to exist through their poems, but poems are a way we convey our experiences to others. Even if the experiences are fictions, perhaps especially if the experiences are fictions, they exist as representations of their authors. These representations, however, are not a substitute for being alive.

I wrote above that poems do not behave themselves. They exhibit a certain autonomy that can be frustrating for their poets, but it is this autonomy that endows the poem with life. Many people are under the impression that a poet decides: I will write a poem about love or history or injustice, etc. What they do not understand is that the greatest virtue a poet possesses is the ability to let a poem happen, to step back, and not to interfere. This is not an argument for free association or complete spontaneity. The role of the poet is much like Socrates's claim to be a philosophical midwife. Our ideas and emotions and everything we have thought or learned are the raw materials the poem uses to bring itself into being. We also have the job of editing. We edit those spots where we haven't done a very good job of being an amanuensis to the poem. Such a poem is not something wrong that needs fixing. We have simply failed to listen as well as we should.

Tomas Tranströmer explained that the poem is a meeting place. He was referring to the meeting of the conscious and the unconscious minds, but it is more than that. Each time the poem meets the reader is a singular event as well. Each time, it speaks to the reader differently because the reader is bringing different experiences to each reading. We are used to seeing reproductions everywhere, so the objects that make up our world can rapidly lose their uniqueness. Reproductions of great paintings, for example, can become icons or memes before we're aware of it. We may think of them in terms of what they purportedly signify rather than what they are. But despite the efforts of unimaginative teachers, the autonomy of the poem keeps asserting itself, demanding that the reader come to the poem without preconceptions. Each reader encounters a different poem.

The autonomy of the poem pulls it in unexpected directions for both the poet and the reader. The poet might have had no idea what kind of poem would appear on the page or might realize the poem wants to take a different shape, perhaps a sonnet or a villanelle. This new form then gives another meaning to the poem. For the reader, the poem may suddenly become a mirror for unrecognized emotions or experiences that had been forgotten. This, then, is the reason to write poems and the reason to read them. We want to encounter what is not ourselves and to discover in that encounter parts of ourselves that had not previously existed.

    The waiter has just brought me a glass of beer and a small bowl of olives. The sun has dropped behind the buildings that border the square. I pull my jacket a little closer and notice the pigeons have flown up to the rooftops.

Madrid, April 18, 2024

Why Poetry?

There is no obvious reason why poetry has been around for so long or why it has assumed its position of importance in so many cultures. Octavio Paz once pointed out that while not every culture had invented prose, all had invented poetry. So, why poems? Stories are easy to understand: they are models of lives, and like our lives, we do not know their meaning until they're completed. (Thank you, Walter Benjamin.) But, poetry, at least lyric poetry, is usually without a clearly defined beginning, middle, and end. Instead, we receive a picture, an image, a kind of unpolished lump of time.

Oddly, that moment the lyric poem embodies holds significance for us. Perhaps, this is because it resembles and is born from the most fundamental mechanism of our own minds: memory. My hypothesis here is limited for its evidence to the way my own mind works. Someday, I will ask a neurologist friend about this, but it's not something I've done yet. If you ask me: what was your childhood like? I am likely to reply with a specific instance, a memory that will seem to stand for what I felt during that time of life. This is not a conscious decision I make; it is the way I remember. Lyric poetry, which brings together thought and emotion, follows the same process.

When I teach poetry-writing to students who don't have much experience of it, often the most difficult problem they face is allowing these moments to emerge in words. Their first impulse is to impose an outcome or an order on the memory to domesticate it, to make it acceptable as a personal history. But, what all poets learn is that these memories and the poems that result from them do not obey us like well-trained dogs. They do not sit when we tell them to or follow us at heel. We cope with this disobedience in various ways. We can embrace it, trying to get it onto the page with as little editing as possible. We can create formal structures using meters, repetitions, rhymes, and other devices to encourage the poem to make its home on our page. We can listen to it to hear what kind of poem it is and how it can be best expressed. What we cannot do is to deny it; we cannot refuse the truthfulness of the experience. The poem does not always make the poet into its hero, and how we come to judge ourselves later may mean nothing to that poetic memory. We have to learn to accept and trust the poems that come to us.

The lyric poem is not there to teach a moral lesson, and we don't write such poems to prove what good people we are. It comes to us as knowledge about ourselves and others that we may not particularly want to know. It has its own agenda, and all we can do is to get it onto the page in a way that retains its freedom. If we are extremely lucky, we will eventually understand that this bundle of words, which is as close as we get to actual memory, is who we are.

How to Write a Love Poem

I'm sorry to disappoint readers who are expecting a set of instructions or a "craft essay," but a love poem that's any good depends on factors that have nothing to do with how skilled we are at marshalling words and images. A love poem begins with emotion. If a poet fakes that emotion, it will likely become painfully obvious before we get too far into the poem. But, what is a "good" love poem? There must be lots of opinions and definitions involved in this, but I only know one: the poem has to convince me that its emotions are so real I can taste them. From that perspective, a love poem is like any other. It creates an experience for the reader that feels true. All the elements of the poem contribute to that reality, or they should be jettisoned. This doesn't mean you have to be in love with a live human being to write a love poem. I remember reading somewhere that Robert Herrick may have made up his beloveds out of whole cloth—and it doesn't matter because his emotions were real, even if their objects were not.

Many years ago when I taught freshman composition, I used to groan when a student would use the cliché "today's society." I'd take the position that the most important things hadn't changed at all. To some extent, this is true of writing love poems as well, but . . . more images and stories are thrown at us now than any other society has ever had to endure. Can you count how many films you've seen in your lifetime? How many tv shows? Then, there are all the songs you've heard? Advertisements? I have no idea how many love stories I've encountered, and I bet no one else does either. As a result of that, and my natural disposition, I'm a pessimist. I know that the beautiful young lovers in the movie who have survived fighting monsters or evil corporations or both will have a completely different challenge changing diapers or mowing the lawn, and I also know that they will grow old, smell bad, and die eventually. What kind of love poem will satisfy readers who share my pessimism? My answer would be: one that acknowledges the contingencies we face as human beings and that can still affirm the value of our feelings.

Shakespeare anticipated this—as he did almost everything else in our lives—when he wrote Sonnet 130:

> My mistress' eyes are nothing like the sun;
> Coral is far more red than her lips' red;
> If snow be white, why then her breasts are dun;
> If hairs be wires, black wires grow on her head.
> I have seen roses damasked, red and white,
> But no such roses see I in her cheeks;
> And in some perfumes is there more delight
> Than in the breath that from my mistress reeks.
> I love to hear her speak, yet well I know
> That music hath a far more pleasing sound;
> I grant I never saw a goddess go;
> My mistress, when she walks, treads on the ground.
>   And yet, by heaven, I think my love as rare
>   As any she belied with false compare.

The only way the poet's love can be believed after centuries of courtier's virtuoso praise is to declare all the ways in which his beloved does not match the usual epithets of love poetry.

This is the same kind of gesture Jack Gilbert makes in "Failing and Flying," when he praises when "love comes to an end," not love's beginning with all its hopes and enthusiasm. He recalls his life with the unnamed beloved—whom we know was Linda Gregg—on a Greek island "while love was fading out of her":

> Every morning she was asleep in my bed
> like a visitation, the gentleness in her
> like antelope standing in the dawn mist.
> Each afternoon I watched her coming back
> through the hot stony field after swimming,
> the sea light behind her and the huge sky
> on the other side of that. Listened to her
> while we ate lunch. How can they say
> the marriage failed?

If Gilbert had given this picture of their life together as a description of the beginning of their relationship, it would have seemed nostalgic and exaggerated, but by praising the end of the marriage, he convinces us of the reality of his feelings.

To put it simply, the best love poems are anti-love poems. They argue against what we expect. They address the complications of love and acknowledge the likelihood of failure. Auden's "Lullaby" tells the beloved, "Lay your sleeping head, my love, / Human on my faithless arm." The poet is only able to invoke blessings on the one who shares his bed because he knows that "Certainty, fidelity / On the stroke of midnight pass / Like vibrations of a bell...." There is a courage in love poems not because we doubt the intentions of the objects of our love but because we doubt our own.

The problem of the reality of a poem often expresses itself as a problem of voice. We must be persuaded by the poem to believe its speaker. While this is a problem of rhetoric, it is also more. The voice of any poem is created by the poet. To acknowledge it as a construction in words is not to lessen its importance or authenticity. There are all sorts of ways in which the world described by the poem should be consistent with our own. The language must be the everyday language of the poet. I'm sure there are still poets who use literary language in their love poems, but we're unlikely to run into their work, and they're likely to remain celibate. Similarly, in the 21st century, baroque diction and a Miltonic pitch may seem freakish rather than real.

To write a love poem today, one that will convince the pessimistic reader, the poet must write with an awareness not only of the transience of love but also of the inevitability of death. We are told by many well-meaning people that love survives death. Religious belief aside, there is no poetic reason whatsoever to give credence to that statement. What might survive death is the representation of love in art and literature. However, this is as much a matter of luck as it is of a poem's profundity.

At this point, I should confess that I am probably the wrong person to write this essay. I cannot recall ever having sat down to write a love poem. I have written a lot of what I think of as love poems, but they have happened almost by accident. I would be writing a poem about whatever I was writing about, usually my own life, and the feelings I had would begin to insert themselves into the poem. I don't think I could have stopped these poems from becoming love poems.

Still, the title here obligates me to give some advice, so I'll try. In the Duino Elegies, Rilke tells us not to attempt to impress the angel with our feelings, rather to tell him of some common thing that is part of our life, and he will stand amazed. This is also how to write a love poem. Writing about the coffee cups the two of you drank from at breakfast or the sunflowers you bought at a kiosk will say more about your life together, or the life you want to have together, than all the delicate abstractions that have come down to us about love or even desire. Faced with the inroads time is sure to make on any happiness, what we will recall are the moments associated with these objects, with small sounds like breath moving over a pillow, or the rough weave of a wool sweater hung over a chair. The fragility of objects and the ephemeral quality of these moments that would otherwise have been lost will write your love poem for you, if you'll let them.

Myths of the Poetry Biz

These days, we click on our Facebook feed, Instagram, or Threads (or even TikTok), and see new publications announced by our friends, acquaintances, even ourselves, and we check to see who has commented on them or who hasn't yet even clicked on them. If this is the current way to measure the worth of a poem, a group of poems, or maybe our own worth, then it's hard not to feel a creeping anxiety. Does all that literary work come down to a certain number of readers clicking "Like"? On discussion groups, the term *poetry biz* circulates as though it's a perfectly natural description. I'm happy that there are so many journals out there where poets can send their work, and for sure, there are many fine poems being written. But, it is the merchandising of poetry and the process of writing it that I find disturbing. The myths that arise out of this merchandising put us in danger of losing the reason why we read and write poetry in the first place.

Before listing several of these myths and at the risk of asking for the reader's unjustified trust, I want to begin with a segue, a passage from an extraordinarily unfashionable poem by an extraordinarily unfashionable poet:

> So here I am, in the middle way, having had twenty years—
> Twenty years largely wasted, the years of *l'entre deux guerres*—
> Trying to use words, and every attempt
> Is a wholly new start, and a different kind of failure
> Because one has only learnt to get the better of words
> For the thing one no longer has to say, or the way in which
> One is no longer disposed to say it. And so each venture
> Is a new beginning, a raid on the inarticulate,
> With shabby equipment always deteriorating

> In the general mess of imprecision of feeling,
> Undisciplined squads of emotion. And what there is to conquer
> By strength and submission, has already been discovered
> Once or twice, or several times, by men whom one cannot hope
> To emulate—but there is no competition—
> There is only the fight to recover what has been lost
> And found and lost again and again: and now, under conditions
> That seem unpropitious. But perhaps neither gain nor loss.
> For us, there is only the trying. The rest is not our business.
> —*T.S. Eliot, from "East Coker."*

Imagine for a moment that a contemporary journal received one of the Four Quartets as a submission. I have little doubt that in most cases it would be rejected by the first reader because: it's too long, the diction is too academic, the first letter of each line is capitalized, the language is not gender-neutral, the subject matter is difficult and elitist, and it excludes many readers because it doesn't represent their social experience. The comments of this imaginary first reader could go on for pages. Regardless of the style of any poet writing today, that poet should be concerned that our apparently flourishing literary world may have an undiagnosed ailment. We may disagree with Eliot's ideas, struggle with some of his poems, and condemn his politics and prejudices, but if we pretend he's not important anymore, we are condemning our own poetry to becoming increasingly trivial.

Consider the warning at the end of Zbigniew Herbert's poem "Why the Classics":

> if art for its subject
> will have a broken jar
> a small broken soul
> with a great self-pity
> what will remain after us
> will be like lovers' weeping
> in a small dirty hotel

when wall-paper dawns
(Trans. by Peter Dale Scott and Czeslaw Milosz)

Herbert could be describing much of contemporary poetry. While there has always been bad or trivial poetry around, what is different here is that after the Second World War, a new myth system grew up that allowed a different kind of literary product to be marketed, profitably, both to the academy and to consumers of popular culture. This product did not need to be measured against the poetry of earlier centuries or cultures, whose authors were deemed either irrelevant or corrupt. Whitman had written, "I celebrate myself," but then, he went on to show how immensely complex that self was. This new poetry also celebrated the self, but it was a "myself-lite," a simplified self, that did not doubt it was free of political, cultural, or moral fault. Its exponents were schooled in MFA programs, which made lots of money for their institutions because there were few scholarships. No one was ever quite sure, though, what to do with the MFA degree or exactly what it certified. Its students—myself among them—graduated, looked around, and realized that the degree did not qualify us for any full-time jobs. We took a deep breath and went on to other things.

Eventually, the internet arrived, and starting a magazine or journal no longer required heavy-duty layout and printing costs and/or ten of your friends standing around to collate and staple. Anyone could be an editor, and there were so many journals that almost every poem could find a home somewhere. The only inconvenience was that even editors need to eat and have a place to sleep. It didn't cost much to publish a digital magazine, but it also didn't pay much either. (Just about every editor I know still has a day job, and often, they put their own money into the magazine.) Moreover, if the online journals weren't free, there wouldn't be many (or perhaps any) readers. So, some unknown enterprising person got the idea to charge the authors a reading fee. This rarely cost very much, except for contest submissions, whose inventor had probably been previously employed by a casino. And, ever since, the system has lumbered along, paid for by the writers who want to see their work published. The identity of the readers of many of these journals is an open question. I suspect it is often family and friends of the contributors and writers who want to become contributors. Sometimes, these are the same.

This is how we ended up with a cultural world turned on its head: with far more writers than readers, with writers paying to be read by editors, and with a reduction in the intellectual, emotional, and social scope of what poetry addresses. Any system or society depends on myths for its identity. This one is no different. For the system to work, writers have to want to be published enough to pay reading fees, workshop fees, craft lecture fees, and manuscript consultation fees, and have to believe various farfetched, but foundational, stories about getting published and what publishing means. Before we can change these myths, we have to recognize that we've bought into them and that they're not true.

Some Myths About Writing and Publishing Poetry:

1. If you thoroughly workshop a poem and incorporate everyone's comments, it will be a better poem.

There is simply no reason to believe that the "wisdom of crowds" applies to poetry. A good lyric poem reflects a single person's experience. It is not written by committee. In fact, to the extent a poem evidences the sensibilities of multiple people, the more homogenized and generic it is likely to become. A poet may, however, find it useful to read a poem out loud to another person or to a group of people. That process allows the writer to hear the poem differently. If some line sounds awkward, reading the poem out loud will direct the poet's attention to that line. The comments of the audience are beside the point. (I should acknowledge here that I've taught a lot of workshops, and I do not exempt these from my criticism of workshops. I try, though, to emphasize to my students, who are incarcerated in Florida state prisons, that the poems are their own and that they have the freedom to decide what is useful and what isn't.)

2. *Editors know more than writers.*

Most editors are heroic individuals who make difficult sacrifices so that the literature they love can find a readership. But, only a few have a special gift for finding the best work among the thousands of submissions they receive. Do the math. Medium-sized journals can receive hundreds of submissions per month. The editors, even if they are great and careful readers, do not have the time to evaluate each submission with much more than a quick glance, and the task of review frequently falls to the least experienced readers available: interns and assistants. The truth is that the editor (assuming the work ever gets to the editor) is unlikely to have any greater sensitivity or knowledge than the writer who submitted the work. A winning lottery ticket is when, through some miracle, an editor happens to spend time with a poem and connects with it. This can happen and sometimes does happen, but we should not expect it to happen. My point is: be grateful when you get good editing, but don't automatically assume that editors are more knowledgeable than you are about what you're trying to accomplish and how to achieve it.

3. *Editors choose the best work.*

Sadly or not, we live in a time where there is little agreement as to what constitutes a good poem. There are probably editors who prefer poems with baroque diction and unusual meters and other editors who prefer poems that have the "authentic" feel of poverty and alienation. Anyone with a free WordPress account can start a magazine. This is certainly liberating, but it is also troubling. If there is no agreement on a literary canon, then how do we know whether our own work is any good? Some editors may be tempted to negotiate this lack of agreement by publishing a tasting menu of work whose only real criterion is that, at worst, it should be unoffensive to most of the journal's potential readers, and at best, it should represent the worldview of many of those readers. *There are exceptions, editors who do their own reading of submissions, have definite tastes, and have a serious love of literature. They are on the endangered-species list, but they do exist.*

4. *Editors are curating a selection of work that fits together to create a whole that is more than the sum of its parts, which is why they reject certain poems.*

Editors do tell themselves this, so maybe it's their own myth. To be fair, they often start off with an idea of a mood, event, or emotion they want to see an issue explore, and certain journals do publish excellent thematic issues. Still, it would be very rare indeed to get an email from an editor that said, "I love this poem so much, and it is so important. The world will be a better place when it is published. However, I can't risk disturbing the perfect balance of work I've already chosen for this issue." I would find that email very hard to believe. Editors may just find it easier to say that the work you submitted doesn't fit this issue than to say, "Sorry, not for me." If an editor really loves a submission and has no place for it, what is to stop said editor from asking the poet if holding it for the next issue is okay?

    5. Editors are genuinely worried they will crush the fragile egos of the poets they reject.

We have all gotten those rejection emails that say, "We are writers too, and we understand how hard it is to have work rejected. Don't let it stop you from writing. Etc." Rejections like these infantilize the poets who receive them. If writers aren't tough to begin with, they had better get tough in a hurry. Rejection is aggravating, but I suspect these overly solicitous emails are really more a way for the editors and staff to feel good about themselves—or at least not to feel bad about themselves—than a way to offer encouragement to poets whose poems have been rejected. (We should also consider the possibility that the template for these emails was originally drafted by someone who had worked in corporate human resources. They have that feel.) *Nota bene*, rudeness or sarcasm, the opposite of the overly solicitous rejection, from an editor is never justified. Regardless how unskilled, politically retrograde, or simply awful a submission may be, an editor always has the simple option of saying, "No thank you." A cousin of the overly solicitous rejection is the we-don't-even-know-what-we-like-or-why-we-like-it rejection. I don't know which I find more offensive. If you don't know what kind of poems you like and why you like them, then why are you publishing a literary journal?

    6. Writers should revise their work if it is rejected.

Most submissions will be rejected. Many writers have the experience of a piece being rejected by numerous small journals and then being picked up by a much larger journal. Why assume that there is something wrong with work that is rejected? Continue to revise as revisions appear good to you, but there is no reason to assume that a rejection means there is something wrong with a poem. *In fact, consider the possibility that rejection means you are writing something unexpected and different.* It may simply be a while before the work will find its audience. A writer has the obligation to make the work into its best possible expression but also has the obligation to believe in the value of the work and to trust it.

    7. *Getting published in as many venues as possible is the goal.*

Good writing is *not* about the quantity of publications. This kind of economic thinking reduces art to business metrics. Look at it this way: nobody gets rich writing poetry, and very few people become famous writing poetry. If your goal is making a lot of money or becoming famous, do something else.

    8. *Prompts make you write great poems.*

If it were that easy, we would all be doing it. Prompts are fine for beginning writers, as are workshops, craft essays, and lectures. But, they are only really useful if you can make them entirely your own and if they coincide with concerns and emotions you are already experiencing. The downside of prompts is that they may lead to boring, trivial poems and to wordplay devoid of real emotion or story.

    9. *Writing every day is the key.*

This is another business import. Yes, if you are going to get a long novel down on paper, you will probably have to write every day, but does that really help poets? Poetry is a mode of writing that requires new ideas and new understandings for each piece, and it is fueled by contradictory feelings, Yeats's "quarrel with ourselves." To be fair, if you don't sit down to write and see what happens, you may be ignoring those poetry-generating feelings, but most often, I hear poets needlessly and neurotically beating themselves up that they don't produce poems on a daily basis.

10. The more craft essays you read, and the more workshops, critiques, and lectures you attend, the better your writing will become.

There is no secret sauce. The skills of writing are learned in two ways, by reading and by writing. Of course, you have to learn to read carefully and to ask the right questions about what you're reading. As for the writing, you have to allow yourself to get into trouble, to write about the things that are difficult and important to you, and then to find your way out of that trouble. Craft lore is unlikely to help. This is because the answer is usually personal. Seriously, what magic do you think clings to the poets who write about craft? They are just like the rest of us, struggling to articulate what we feel but can't quite name. (Remember that passage from Eliot?) The rules of writing poetry are descriptive, not prescriptive. Thomas Hardy and Shakespeare both, at least once, mixed metaphors. (I confess that I can't remember where Hardy did it, but I remember that he did.) They made it work. Still, if you don't know the rules, you won't know when you're breaking them.

Please don't construe these myth-criticisms as nostalgia for the good old days of stamped, self-addressed envelopes and physical slush piles filling up otherwise empty rooms. Those days may have been old, but they were not good. A lot of great work went unnoticed, and the cost of all those stamps and envelopes was not insignificant. It's also amazing to have so many venues today for poetry. However, this doesn't relieve us of the need to question what we're doing and how our choices affect us and our work. If we are going to participate with our words, our time, and our money in the *poetry biz*, we should do it with as few unexamined myths as possible.

I began these thoughts with Eliot because, whatever else he may have been, he was not trivial. He insisted on poetry connecting with something larger than self-expression. That connection is rare and not easy to market. We won't find it in workshops and critiques, and it won't be learned from craft essays. Yet, the possibility of encountering it may well have been what drew us to poetry in the first place. I am aware that the concept of the poet as someone whose words enlarge our world is one of the oldest myths, exactly the one that gave rise to Plato's hostility to poets. It is certainly easy for the prophetic to slip into the merely spontaneous or to the ruminations of bloated egos. At the same time, it is not wrong for us to want more and to ask it of ourselves and others—just as it's not wrong to embrace the unfashionable.

WRITING ABOUT WHAT'S NO LONGER HERE

So many poems are written about death, but it is the nature of language to describe something that can be described or to reason about abstractions. Death is neither, and that presents a problem for poetry. When anyone dies, there is an absence, one life is missing from all the ways it interacted with other lives. Further, that life is now fixed in place as a memory. Whatever it was is what it will be. Memories may soften or harden, but the life itself is beyond changing. To romanticize or sentimentalize a dead person's life is to lie about it. We owe the dead the duty of being truthful to the facts of the life that was here.

Joseph Brodsky once told his seminar at Columbia that elegies are usually about their author, not the person being elegized. Even Auden, whom Brodsky praised for keeping himself out of his elegies, weighs his subjects by the posthumous effects of their lives. The manner of their deaths are generally irrelevant, subordinate in Yeats's case to the weather. Their missteps in life are also subordinated to what they become in death, how they exist in collective memory and thought. Auden's elegies were great, for sure, but they border on the apologetic. They have a bad conscience. The twentieth century mind, much less the twenty-first, was suspicious of Aristotle's great-souled man and suspicious of the subjects of elegies. Auden negotiated those suspicions and struggled with them himself. He couldn't decide whether time would be generous enough to pardon writers for all their flaws as persons. For this reason, he is the end of an elegiac tradition.

Poems about death don't start or stop at elegy, but to write directly about death is to mythologize what cannot be comprehended. This mythologizing is an extremely useful tool, but it should not be conflated with what's true. What we know about death is that a person, and eventually all persons, comes to a stop. A person who joked, ate, drank, made love, worked, got angry, had conflicted emotions, took actions in the world—that person ended. Auden says of Yeats that "he became his admirers." While this does describe how a major poet enters and influences the minds and lives of others, I doubt Auden thought of this as a kind of afterlife, and it avoids the fact of death itself.

John Donne writes about it best, with a good conscience if not exactly a modern one, "Any man's death diminishes me, because I am involved in mankind." From the standpoint of those of us who continue to live, death is exactly that diminishment that Donne describes. The other's death makes our own death not a distant possibility or a mythologized state, but an inevitable reality, the syllogistic logic that says: all men are mortal, Caius is a man, therefore Caius is mortal. Tolstoy's Ivan Ilyich is reminded of this and denies that he is Caius. The gap between logic and experience is a huge one, but for Donne, that gap doesn't exist. And, to read him the way he wished to be read is to feel that gap vanish as you read.

Nonetheless, we cannot imagine death itself. We cannot imagine the end of our being ourselves. We can, though, imagine the effects a life has on others even past death. What Brodsky complained of in poets, writing their elegies about themselves, may not be such a bad thing, or at least not an unproductive one. It is possible that all poems are elegies for their poet. We expect poems to have an effect on readers, and poets hope to continue to exist by creating that effect. But, this is also a form of mythologizing. The poem is not the poet. It is analogous to a belief that if you are buried and a tree takes nourishment from your corpse, you somehow continue to live in the tree—a not-very-reassuring thought.

In mathematics, the invention of the zero to stand for nothing allowed for levels of calculation not previously available. Naming something through language, however, does not mean we know anything about what's been named, and attempting even to name non-existence is to be reminded how inadequate language is to fact. Poetry is no more adequate to the fact of death than any other form of language, but paradoxically poets are drawn to addressing it. Death is unspeakable, but we somehow continue to speak of it.

POETRY AND THE IMAGE

The image is at the heart of poetry. Without the image, there can be music on the one hand and speech on the other, but not poetry. This is because poetry originates in the human impulse to control the uncontrollable by recreating it. Examples are the cave art that depicts successful hunts (as far as I know, there is no cave art depicting unsuccessful hunts) or when Yahweh reveals himself in a burning bush and Moses asks his name because knowing the name of a god gives you power over that god. Similarly, love poetry conjures the beloved. Sappho asks Aphrodite to help her win her beloved, and Neruda re-creates Josie Bliss in "Widower's Tango." He goes so far as to describe her making water behind the house, a "silvery, persistent honey." (Donald D. Walsh tr.)

The image is central to the act of conjuring. Sometimes in poetry we conjure the past, remember the dead, say to them what we didn't say, or said badly, when they were alive. We are told the Orphic mysteries involved the phrase: "As above, so below." One world mirrors the other. The poem is a counter-world that mirrors this one, that challenges its reality. In the process, it affirms the integrity of the self, the self's right to re-make the world, to refuse to be reduced to statistics or biological destiny. In order to create a world strong enough to stand against the forces that all-too-convincingly tell us that we're unimportant, we make images, pictures of the world we devise. If those pictures are real enough, the reader will say, "Yes, it's exactly like that!"

The rhetoric of argument, discourse, exists within the day-to-day world. It involves the maneuvers of armies, the building of schools and prisons, the regulation of trade, even the regulation of ideas, which is perhaps one way to think of philosophy. There is no disputing the magnitude of that outside world or how it can crush us in a thousand different ways. Against it, we have poetry, where the poet tells us to listen to this story, this song, let these pictures enter through our ears and make us look at things differently. Stevens described poetry as "a violence from within that protects us from a violence without. It is the imagination pressing back against the pressure of reality." To be clear, poetry does not stop bullets or convince citizens to defy demagogues and politicians to behave themselves when no one is looking, but it struggles to create a reality that affirms our dignity as individual selves even in those moments when it despairs of its own ability to change anything.

That is the ironic aspect of poetry. It offers us most when it grieves the hardest, when it acknowledges that Orpheus cannot bring back Eurydice from Hades, that dictators make their omelets with the broken eggs of the bodies and minds they subjugate, that human beings get old and die. In other words, the articulation of despair and pain places that despair and pain within a different context, as part of a story where the sufferer has a voice and will be heard. In this, poetry is much like prayer, and sometimes the line between the two is blurred. The person praying knows that the value of prayer is not just how effective it is in convincing a deity to fulfill the prayer. It is a statement that affirms the value of the one praying and, therefore, answers itself. Plotinus called prayer "the flight of the alone to the alone." So, the value of the poem is not its ability to change the world, but rather its ability to change our response to the world.

The image, then, is more than a technical device of poetry. Our view of the world is always a singular view, limited, deficient. We see this side of the tree or that one, but not both sides at once. We cannot look up and down at the same time. If we are trying to create a reality, our tools are what we perceive, the tactile things, the cat's fur beneath our hands, the burn of the sun on our shoulders. This is what empowers our poems, makes them real enough to do their job. The image moves quickly in our minds, just the way a perception of the world moves when we're walking down the street or lifting a spoon to our lips. The images we present are the familiar images of our own perceptions, what we see. As a result, readers see them as well.

The image is the re-creation of the exterior world. It is also a subversion of that world, taking what in discourse is a weakness, the partiality and subjectivity of our perception, and making it into a strength. And, it transgresses boundaries. Idols are frowned upon in western religions not just because they reduce the unseeable to the seen and not just because they were ineffective—idols like poems can't change the exterior world—but because they were an assertion of power on the part of the worshippers. The image of the god could be manipulated, smeared with honey or calves' blood to try to make sure the worshippers got what they wanted. While the image in poetry does not change the exterior world, it does manipulate the reader's response to that world, and it does offer the possibility of an alternative world. It is primitive in this way and takes us back to rites of magic performed by torchlight in caves. Images are also dangerous because they are not limited to just one meaning. They can have different meanings in different contexts or to different readers. We can create them but not necessarily control them. They tend to make a poem go off in its own direction, one that we have no choice but to accept. In this as well, they are at the heart of poetry.

TRANSLATION AND THE POETIC

There is a widely held view that the translation of poetry is doomed from the beginning. Frost left us his famous line that poetry is what is lost in the translation, and Hannah Arendt wrote of Auden that she knew he was a great poet because his work did not translate. While both Frost and Arendt are deities for me, I disagree with them on this issue. When Pound translated Li Po's "The River Merchant's Wife: A Letter," he could not reproduce or even approximate the formal qualities of classic Chinese poetry. Instead, he chose to use cadenced verse with irregular lines, suggesting a kind of transparency of meaning. This suggestion may or may not be an illusion, but I am concerned here with what kind of poem it produced. Here is Pound's version of Li Po:

> While my hair was still cut straight across my forehead
> I played about the front gate, pulling flowers.
> You came by on bamboo stilts, playing horse,
> You walked about my seat, playing with blue plums.
> And we went on living in the village of Chōkan:
> Two small people, without dislike or suspicion.
> At fourteen I married My Lord you.
> I never laughed, being bashful.
> Lowering my head, I looked at the wall.
> Called to, a thousand times, I never looked back.
>
> At fifteen I stopped scowling,
> I desired my dust to be mingled with yours
> Forever and forever, and forever.
> Why should I climb the look out?
>
> At sixteen you departed,
> You went into far Ku-tō-en, by the river of swirling eddies,

And you have been gone five months.
The monkeys make sorrowful noise overhead.

You dragged your feet when you went out.
By the gate now, the moss is grown, the different mosses,
Too deep to clear them away!
The leaves fall early this autumn, in wind.
The paired butterflies are already yellow with August
Over the grass in the West garden;
They hurt me. I grow older.
If you are coming down through the narrows of the river Kiang,
Please let me know beforehand,
And I will come out to meet you
As far as Chō-fū-Sa.

It's certainly possible to claim that such cadenced verse is not poetry, only prose cut into lines, but that misses the obvious point that over a hundred years of readers have read it as poetry. Certainly, something is going on, and it is that "something" I find most interesting. It is also possible to respond that the readers are receiving Pound, not Li Po. I am not particularly troubled by this objection because it applies to every translation, even ones where various formal qualities of the original text can be approximated.

It is also important here to note that the formal qualities of Pound's cadences in the Cathay translations do not bear much resemblance to Whitman's cadenced lines or other examples in English of earlier poets who eschewed regular meter and rhyme. He was doing something new that changed what readers perceived as poetry. He was locating what was "poetic" about his translations of Chinese poetry in something more subtle than a regular pattern of sounds with minor variations. This is not to say he was any clearer about what he was doing than we are now, trying to figure it out. His definition of an image is a good example: "An 'Image' is that which presents an intellectual and emotional complex in an instant of time." In that definition, he avoids the common and traditional sense of the image merely as a visual representation of something, a picture. It's fair for us to ask why.

Clearly, Pound believed he was translating a poem, that he was bringing over a verbal construction in Chinese that compressed and conveyed ideas and feelings into an equivalent construction in English. While it was impossible to approximate the formal qualities of the poem, approximating the pictorial aspects of the representation was a possibility. This leaves open the question whether the pictorial aspects meant the same thing to the original readers. Pound seems to have believed they did. Even if he failed on this or that specific, something is being conveyed from one language to another, and that something continues to move many of his readers. The "something" is the poetic. The problem is that it remains elusive.

Pound's Imagist period only lasted a few years. While he may have blamed Amy Lowell's takeover of the movement, he was probably already chaffing at its limitations. Whatever it is that makes a poem a poem is broader in scope than an image, even if images form a large part of the poem and are highly suggestive of ideas and feelings.

In a poem's original language, the qualities of sound are often responsible for the effect of the poem. In Tennyson's "Tithonus," Tithonus watches the dawn slowly emerge from his goddess lover:

> Once more the old mysterious glimmer steals
> From thy pure brows, and from thy shoulders pure,
> And bosom beating with a heart renew'd.
> Thy cheek begins to redden thro' the gloom,
> Thy sweet eyes brighten slowly close to mine,
> Ere yet they blind the stars, and the wild team

Which love thee, yearning for thy yoke, arise,
And shake the darkness from their loosen'd manes,
And beat the twilight into flakes of fire.

I doubt that translations of these lines would convey their poem-ness very well, but the poetic is certainly found here. It is not simply that the noise of the poem is beautiful and filled with longing and awe. The sounds of the line are instrumental in generating the poem's reality. We believe them and are drawn into the moment because of them. Frost and Arendt may be right when it comes to translating this type of poem, but Pound's belief in the capability of the poetic to be translated is also correct.

A good friend of mine was once criticized in graduate school for believing that when he asked a question that he was supposed to answer it. Like my friend, I think it's important at least to try. To the extent that we perceive or respond to translations of poetry as poems, similar to our response to poems in our own language, we know "the poetic" is present even if unlocated. To me, the poet who seems to translate best is Cavafy. I write this without the slightest knowledge of modern Greek, but I know that I have never come across a translation of Cavafy into English that did not affect me. That includes prose translations. Some of his translators, of course, are better than others, but his treatment of the subject matter in his work, whether the poems are set contemporaneously or in the Hellenic past, survives regardless. This may seem odd because I'm told that he utilizes both meter and a blend of katharevousa and demotic forms of Greek that would probably defy English translation.

I can't write about Cavafy without an example. In "The God Abandons Antony," he has a set piece that doesn't seem promising. Yet, it works. For my purposes, I will choose the very understated translation by Edmund Keeley and Philip Sherrard.

> When suddenly, at midnight, you hear
> an invisible procession going by
> with exquisite music, voices,
> don't mourn your luck that's failing now,
> work gone wrong, your plans
> all proving deceptive—don't mourn them uselessly.
> As one long prepared, and graced with courage,
> say goodbye to her, the Alexandria that is leaving.
> Above all, don't fool yourself, don't say
> it was a dream, your ears deceived you:
> don't degrade yourself with empty hopes like these.
> As one long prepared, and graced with courage,
> as is right for you who proved worthy of this kind of city,
> go firmly to the window
> and listen with deep emotion, but not
> with the whining, the pleas of a coward;
> listen—your final delectation—to the voices,
> to the exquisite music of that strange procession,
> and say goodbye to her, to the Alexandria you are losing.

Like Pound's image, this poem is "an intellectual and emotional complex in an instant of time." Cavafy does not tell us who is speaking to Antony, urging him, a worshipper of Bacchus, to a tragic nobility that rises above his ending. The speaker doesn't disparage the sensual world in which Antony has lived and does not mention his military exploits. What the speaker says to Antony could be said to anyone. It is the reverse of Rilke's "Archaic Torso of Apollo" with its "There is no part that does not see you. You must change your life." It is too late for Antony to change anything. All he can do is affirm the choices he's made. The speaker, for the fiction of the poem, is Antony's own voice, speaking to himself. It is also Cavafy speaking to himself.

The poem here, which survives translation and the stripping away of whatever poetic devices it had in Greek, is located in the moment of reality created by the speaker's voice. Think of it as an intersection between the setting of the fictional moment or, more simply, the story, the interior monologue, which is the voice, and the recognition this intersection summons in our minds as we read: this is how we speak, or should speak, to ourselves.

I am not suggesting that this is the only kind of poem that survives translation, but more generally, what survives translation in poems that move us is the reality of an experience or moment recreated in the receiving language. The poetic as an entity exists. It doesn't require the formal elements we associate with poetry, although those elements may generate or define the structure of the poem and in some cases are essential to our understanding of the poem.

As readers in the 21st century, we are distrustful of voice and of language itself. We have been taught that voice is artifice, a construct, not a true expression of the consciousness of a person. I don't want to argue with that, only to say that it's irrelevant. All that we make is artifice. What is significant is the effect that what we make creates. That is the transmission of the poetic. We are moved, made to feel and see differently, by what appears real to us. For sure, it is a constructed reality, but one that must be true to our own sense of the world or we will reject it.

Even if we take a nominalist position and say that the poetic does not exist as an entity but only as various instances of experience, the experience of the poem happens nonetheless, and we have to account for it. Translation proves to us that something is being transmitted that is independent, at least to some extent, from its linguistic origins. Some poems are capable of bringing over to another language a reality that moves us. We believe the voices they create, and it is in the presence of such voices and in the consciousnesses they imply that we find the poem.

Prose Poems

There is something feisty, perhaps even fist-like, about prose poems. Maybe it's the oxymoron not only in the name "prose poem" but in the object itself, usually a few sentences cobbled together in a stubby paragraph that dares the reader to claim it's not a poem. Of course, there are longer Paris-Spleen-style prose poems that challenge in a different way. They will tell us a story of sorts but with our understanding that this is not a fiction whose main purpose is to engage us in its exploration of character and plot. Something else is going on.

When a reader typically approaches a poem, whether it is recited or read, the reader understands that the words are intended to give access to something unusual, perhaps the state of mind of the poet experiencing a strong emotion or a foundational story of a people or a religion. The reader who expects revelation and receives instead The Wall Street Journal is likely to be disappointed. (I have to admit here that I know an accountant who argues to me that tax returns are poetry, but I remain unconvinced.)

Let's begin with a working understanding of the term "prose poem," not as a definition or even a description to fit all examples, just a hypothesis to serve as a hilltop from where we can look at the landscape. The prose poem, like other poems, purports to give us the access I mentioned above. However, the form it takes announces that certain features often employed by poetry will not be found here. If there is measure, it is the measure of lightly cadenced prose, or it may avoid any kind of musicality in its sounds. The emphasis is also unlikely to fall on unusual imagery. More often than not, the prose poem will avoid Andre Breton's convulsive beauty. Its most noticeable feature may be how the voice of the poem is created by its syntax, its diction, and its thought or story.

This is not a form for those who view poetry as a game played with words. In that sense, there is something puritanical about prose poetry as well. The accident of two words at the end of their respective lines having a certain combination of consonants and vowels is disdained by the prose poet, as are the alternating stresses so often found in English. The purity of the prose poet lies in the use of words as they exist in their ordinary, spoken habitat. While the prose poet may throw in an exotic word or a phrase from a distant language, it is usually for purposes of verisimilitude. Even traditional poems set in a country in another hemisphere will often employ such fragments; the prose poem does as well, but not as ornament. Rather, the prose poem seeks a reality in all the words it employs.

The prose poem may be the purest kind of poetry because it tells us in essence: "Ignore the extraneous stuff, the accidents of language and interesting noise. Here, you will find a world." Its paragraph is a rectangular window through which we see something essential: Jean Follain exploring a particular day in a village in France in 1914, Max Jacob's autobiographical dislocations, or Robert Hass, in "A Story About the Body," locating the precise moment when a young composer discovers his own romantic cowardice.

The modern prose poem is a creation of 19th-century France, but in the 20th and 21st centuries, its American variations have tilted more toward narrative. Is there a difference between "flash fiction" and prose poetry? If there is, it exists in the author's intention as to how the work should be considered, to what purpose it's addressed. At one point, Octavio Paz explained that poetry embraces a multiplicity of meanings and is at the far end of a language continuum where discourse, which seeks a singular meaning, is at the other. The prose poem, somewhat ironically, can exist at the multiplicity end or in the domain of fiction, which lies somewhere in the middle. While the prose poem dispenses with the ornament of poetic forms and devices—which are all techniques for achieving the otherness of poetry, poetry's estrangement from discourse—prose poetry still seeks out its own otherness. For readers of prose poetry, poetry is not some form of higher enjoyment meant to assure us how different we are from the common herd; rather, it is an epiphany of the objective reality of the world as we experience it.

I remember once spending an afternoon with a reproduction of Sesshū Tōyō's *Long Scroll*, then driving to the supermarket to buy whatever I was going to eat that night for dinner. On the way to the market, all the trees I saw looked like paintings by Sesshū. I was not hallucinating, and the trees hadn't changed in any way. They had simply become real to me in a different way. The world revealed to us by prose poetry is much the same.

The Impulse to Publish

There have been great writers who barely published during their lifetimes. For me, Emily Dickinson is one of the best examples. I'm fascinated by her restraint and confidence. She, like the rest of us, must have understood how many manuscripts end up in dumpsters, fires, or landfills, and how legendary manuscripts, such as Bruno Schultz's *The Messiah*, have been destroyed in wars. She understood these things happen, but she didn't seem to care. We comfort ourselves and attribute it to shyness, some psychological condition, or editors' failures to recognize her work, but these thoughts are possibly just to avoid awareness of our own narcissism and irrational hope for praise.

There are many thousands of literary magazines and journals in the United States alone, and the rest of the world is quickly catching up. Who reads them all? No one could possibly have the time to sit down with a stack each day. Then, there are the books published by small or independent publishers or self-published. Has anyone counted? Truth: we are drowning in our own words. There are many more writers than readers, and the writers—I include myself here— spend much of the limited time we're given on this planet submitting our poems, stories, and memoirs wherever we can submit them. If a new journal opens in India, you can be certain American contributors will overwhelm the editors with submissions. Truth: journals exist to publish writers more than to be read by readers. The economic realities of publishing make this conclusion unavoidable. Unless a journal is supported by a university or has been left an endowment or is supported by the generosity of its editors, it charges a reading fee. It will also likely have publishing contests with more substantial fees. If literary magazines depended on subscribers and purchasers, very few would exist.[1]

What is it that makes so many of us expend so much effort to publish when what we write will, for the most part, be read only by other writers published in a particular journal or by those who seek to be published in that journal? Is there a drive to be published? Diotima told Socrates that all men desire immortality. This desire seems to exist irrespective of gender. Women writers, with the exception of Ms. Dickinson, are afflicted just as much as men. In the time before general literacy, written words possessed a kind of permanence. If humans could not live forever, then perhaps their words could. But, in a world overfull of digital information, what could possibly make us believe that our words still possess this permanence?

It is a very different experience to read what we write in manuscript than to read it in print. When words are in print, they seem to exist independently of the mind that created them. They are out in the world for others to praise or disdain, to gather reactions on social media sites, or even to be reviewed, *i.e.*, to become themselves the subject of others' words. I'd speculate that our mental and experiential worlds as expressed in words exhibit an impulse toward autonomy, an impulse for which we have antithetical feelings. We are afraid of the responses we may receive and the self-knowledge we may encounter. The poems may have taken their poets to places they did not expect to go.

The poems are at once us and not-us. This is especially evident when we write in formal poetry. There,

---

[1] This brief departure to the bottom of the page is to thank those sturdy friends who read our work for no other reason than the pleasure of doing so. It does still happen, and they are much appreciated.

what we will say is determined, at least in part, by what can be said in our given language. Certain words will have a certain number of syllables; others will not. Certain accents will fall in a certain pattern; different words will have a different pattern. In English certain words will rhyme; in other languages, the words that mean something similar will not. Joseph Brodsky used to talk in his seminars about how the language writes the poem, and he was not entirely wrong. Perhaps the urge to see our work in print stems from a need to externalize these verbal creations, to remove them from ourselves so that we can encounter them as something fully different.

Homeric Greeks externalized their strong emotions. These emotions and their consequences were the work of gods. In the Iliad, Agamemnon apologizes to Achilles, saying that Ate blinded him. We moderns treat our feelings as something that happens internally. This is a heavy burden for an individual to bear, and as such, it may result in a poem. The poem may have the effect of externalizing the state of being that produced it, but for most of us, this is not enough. We need to publish, to see that state not only converted into language but fixed on a printed or digital page that is now beyond our recall or control. This is why we are willing to spend so much of our time and resources on publication, with only a fragile hope that our poems will survive their authors.

As you can see, for all the awful and disdainful things I can say about publishing and those of us who attempt to publish our writing, in the end I have to concede it is a noble enterprise. It's an expression of something deeper than the will to obtain economic security or perhaps even happiness. This is the will to make ourselves other than ourselves, to separate ourselves from our experience of events and feelings in order to recreate that experience in words and then to put those words out into the world to go their own way. I would like to say this action requires faith that our efforts will be rewarded, but I don't believe that. We would still try to publish even if we knew the world was ending next week. We might laugh and dismiss it as habit, but it's more than that. This urge to make external what had once existed only as an internal flutter of neurons is something fundamentally human.

The urge I'm describing is greater than a drive toward self-expression, and what we write is greater than the sum of our anxieties, phantasies, or emotional deficits. Even in free verse or prose poetry, the language exerts its pressure and creates both the expression and the boundaries of the expression, and in return, we contribute to the language and add to what can be said. None of this happens without publication.

As much as I admire Emily Dickinson's reticence, her refusal to be "advertised," I can't help thinking how much poorer we would be without her poems, how much less we would understand those states of being she knew better than anyone. From #372 ("After great pain, a formal feeling comes—"):

> This is the Hour of Lead—
> Remembered, if outlived,
> As Freezing persons, recollect the Snow—
> First—Chill—then Stupor—then the letting go—

If our countless literary magazines and our even-more-countless submissions allow for four lines as good as those to be preserved against time, it's all been worth it.

Saving Poetry?

I read an article recently where the author celebrated how certain poets had saved American poetry from being the property of "academic" poets. The author was not a polemicist on a rant but was ecstatic at the energy of our current poetry, so the names of the villainous academic poets went unspoken, in a kind of Harry Potter way. Precisely because they weren't named, I immediately tried to figure out who these academic poets were. However, I hit a quick dead end. I couldn't think of any poets I knew who would consider themselves "academic," and this worried me even more. There is an old saying in poker that if you can't see who the sucker is at the table, the guy who will walk away at the end of the evening with empty pockets, then you are probably that guy. *Am I an academic poet?* It sounds like a terminal diagnosis: you are doomed to have your books stuck on the dustiest shelf in the library. No one will read them, and your only hope will be that the entire civilization will be wiped out and only your tattered pages buried in the ruins will be left.

To fend off this apocalyptic vision, I tried to think about what we mean when we call someone an "academic poet." Certainly, there are hundreds, if not thousands, of poets who teach at colleges and universities. My guess is that absolutely none would self-identify as an "academic poet." Or, does the term just mean somebody who died fifty or more years ago? Did they, upon dying, automatically become academic? Perhaps I was drawing my circle in too restrictive a fashion. Maybe what makes a poet academic is actually that writer's subject matter. If your poem contains a reference to grail myths or Arthurian legends, does that make you fit the category?

(Confession: I did write a poem once about Sir Bedivere selling insurance in Iowa and reminiscing over wings and beer about King Arthur killing a giant, but I never thought of that one as particularly pleasing to professors.) Are references to history, philosophy, or classical art off limits now to poets? I don't think so because the author of the anxiety-producing article seemed to like John Ashbery. This left me with only form to consider, and it can't be that iambic pentameter or rhymed poems are forbidden because too many decidedly non-academic poets have rediscovered formal poetry in the last ten years or so. John Murillo, for example, is one of the most formally exciting poets I've read.

Somewhere in these considerations, I realized that the last poet I'd seen photographed in a tweed jacket and with a pipe in his mouth was Hyam Plutzik—the photo snapped somewhere in the 1950's or earlier—and if you've read his work, you'll realize he was fascinatingly experimental in his language and thought, tweed jacket or not. Or, take Stanley Kunitz. I studied at Columbia with him almost forty years ago. He had refused tenure offers just about everywhere he'd ever taught because he didn't want to be identified with the academy, but maybe Kunitz—regardless of his left-wing politics and painfully beautiful poems—is the kind of poet from whom we have been somehow saved. He was for sure learned. The story goes that he and Theodore Roethke used to play a game where one would challenge the other with a single line of obscure poetry and the one challenged would have to name the poet who wrote it, the title of the poem, and the year it was written. Apparently, being phenomenally well-read doesn't prevent a person from being a great poet, but does it make that poet "academic"?

I recall how when I worked for a law firm in Washington, DC and one of the nastier partners wanted to disparage something I'd drafted, he would refer to it as "academic." (I probably should have disclosed in the first paragraph above that I have some graduate degrees.) It was an easy put-down, and I think it's an easy put-down in poetry as well. There is no one style or subject matter for poetry that is better than all the gazillion others. The only criterion is what works in a particular time and place. If there are academic poets today, they are near invisible. The big commercial publishers publish celebrities and Nobel prize winners—if they publish poetry at all. There is no cabal of "academic poets" reserving poetic laurels and cushy jobs for each other, and there never really has been. For hundreds of years (if not longer), poets have flattered themselves that they are in revolt against whatever has just come before. Sometimes, stylistically this has been true, but most of the time, they were just clearing ground for themselves by pushing aside the poets they'd read most closely. (My more "academic" readers will hear the ghost of Harold Bloom rattling the dishes in my cupboard to show approval.) For the same reason, Octavio Paz defined modernism as "a tradition against itself." Whatever is modern now is against whatever was modern yesterday. Some academics thought they had solved that problem by creating "postmodernism." I did a quick online search of definitions of "postmodern poetry" and found no general agreement on what it was or what the term meant. There were some examples of the "language poets," but they retreated into a justified irrelevance sometime back during the last century. If they were the academics threatening poetry, they were rapidly dispatched because very few people ever found them interesting to read.

This leaves us, academics and non-academics, in a predicament. Is the poetry being written now in rebellion against any predecessors? Should it be? While it's common and usually misguided to think we occupy a unique position in history, we can still acknowledge some distinctions. Goethe pointed out that his period was the first to have access to all the other, earlier periods and to literature translated from many other languages, that he lived in a time of "world literature." What was true for him is even more true for us. The size of our poetic world is so grand that any specific style or group shrinks in proportion and importance. The other factor is acceleration. As I mentioned, nothing stays modern for long, or postmodern. Before a poetic rebellion could be successful, time would already have rendered the previous ruling class antiquated if not entirely irrelevant. How are we supposed to define ourselves in such a world?

This is why it may be time to stop defining by opposition and to adopt a new stance toward our literary history. I suggest—and I write this timidly because I am aware of the multitude of problems and personalities we'd be taking on—that we consider a new kind of classicism. Czeslaw Milosz set up a contest in poetry between the classical and the real. It was a useful distinction because it emphasized how important reality is to the making of poetry. For him, "classical" referred to structure and tradition, and "reality" was that pressure of the immediate that forces us to respond and to include the world in our poems. I mean something quite different. The poems that move us, going back to the beginnings of Western European civilization and even earlier, have certain features in common. First, they are full of life as it's being lived at the time. Second, regardless of the form in which they're written, they are formally memorable. Third, the poems—even the epics—contain a human voice. They are not "author functions." Whitman understood this when he told us, his readers and descendants, "Camerado, this is no book; / Who touches this touches a man." If a poem fulfills these criteria, then with a little luck, it's capable of becoming a classic, and whether the poet who wrote it was an academic or a revolutionary doesn't matter.

Defending Love & Nature

File this under fascinating-but-disturbing news: I read yesterday that an editor of a prominent journal, one I respect and enjoy reading, has announced to the world that poets should never submit love poems to his journal and only rarely submit poems about nature. Of course, it is his magazine, and he can and should publish or not publish whatever he likes. Moreover, what he likes is often excellent by any standards. With those disclaimers in place, I believe he's wrong.

It's not clear to me what to characterize as a "love poem." All Hallmark, soppy, and sentimental verse aside, how do we distinguish between poems that traditionally celebrate a beloved from other poems of desire, fantasy, and loss? Grown-ups know that life is finite, and the proclamation that love conquers death is not particularly convincing. Poems that are written with this knowledge are easy to distinguish from greeting cards. They often question every premise of love and desire, and if they perform this interrogation well, we as readers may find ourselves looking beyond a few abstract nouns and experiencing the poem as real perceptions: sweat, skin, the texture of hair, the quarter-moon of a fingernail, even the damp spot on the mattress.

Is this kind of questioning of emotional states off limits to poets? Are poets supposed to say there have been too many love poems, too much information, too many public displays of affection? Are we moving toward a new decorum in poetry, where love and desire can't exist outside of irony or victimization? This would be a loss for many reasons, but perhaps the most important is that love poems are a way other people become real to us. A love poem often tells us far more about the speaker than it does about the person the speaker loves. Sometimes, the poem can also be the occasion for ruthless introspection. I think about Auden's magnificent "Lullaby," which announces the limits of his love in its opening lines: "Lay your sleeping head, my love, / Human on my faithless arm...."

As for nature poems, in the middle of the 20th century the West Coast poets (Snyder, Rexroth, et al) who wrote poems set in the Sierras were derided as poets who only wrote about "bear shit in the woods." An intimate knowledge of the natural world is hard to come by these days. I envy those poets who have spent enough time in that world to have such knowledge, and I certainly don't want to be denied their poetry. In the 1980s, I was an editorial assistant at a prominent review, where I begged and pleaded that the magazine publish poems submitted by Alaskan homesteader John Haines, poems that had been buried in the slush pile for 6 months. Sadly, I was not successful.

What does it say about us as a culture that important editors (the one I reference above is not alone) have decided that they will not publish poems about two areas of experience that poets have explored for thousands of years? This is a very different demand from Andre Breton's "Beauty will be convulsive, or it will not be at all," or Pound's "Make it new." This implies that the good poets, the ones these editors seek for their pages, should only write (or only submit) not-love poems and not-nature poems.

It takes work to imagine what such poems would have in common, but it occurs to me that they would turn away from the physicality of the world, from trees and rocks as well as fingers and lips. They would be poems about cell phones not turkey buzzards, collapsing buildings not palm fronds or swamps in Minnesota. Perhaps they would exist as mature considerations of history and language or elegant personal narratives of loneliness and isolation. I have nothing against poems like those, but I can see no reason why we should give up love poems and nature poems as a condition of reading other types of poetry. It doesn't speak well for a country or an epoch when editors reject any kind of poetry out of hand. If nothing else, it means abandoning those subjects to sentimental or commercial projects, and our sense of what it means to be a person will inevitably be the less for that abandonment.

Finally, I have not named the editor who declared love or nature poems out of bounds for submission because I hope his statement won't be noticed, that some brilliant poet will send him a love poem so emotionally real and complex that he will change his mind entirely. It could happen.

Ten Things I Learned as a Guest Editor

I was recently asked to guest edit an issue of a literary magazine. For me, this was a first, and I suspect that the editor, who is a good friend, may have wanted to teach me a few lessons about what it's like to be on the other side of the submissions process. OK, I get it. Reading manuscripts is seriously hard work. We capped at 200 submissions, and most submissions had 3 poems each. So, approximately 600 poems later, I understand a little of what regular editors go through every 3 months. My job was to be the first reader of these poems on Submittable and to give a thumbs up to the ones I thought should be accepted. As far as I know, my friend—the real editor—mostly went along with my judgments.

Did I make mistakes? Probably. Maybe even more than probably. All I can do is apologize and tell you that there are lots of stories about great poems being rejected. If you believe in your work and I rejected it, send it to other magazines. Someone else may recognize qualities that I missed.

Beyond realizing how difficult it is to edit a magazine and how fallible my judgment might ultimately be, I did learn or was reminded of things that will influence my own approach to submitting poems and may even be of some help to other writers. *However, these are not rules.* They are simply thoughts that crossed my mind while I was reading submissions or thinking about them later, and *they are simply my thoughts, not policies of any magazine or editor.* Not only should you feel free to disagree with them, but on another occasion, I might disagree with them myself.

1. Most people who submit poems have amazing credentials, and it doesn't matter. There are so many

prizes and important magazines out there, it's not easy to impress anybody. Also, no one has the time (or inclination) to check whether the credentials listed are real. The time is better spent reading the submitted poems, so keep those bios short.

    2. A large percentage of poems are proficient. Submittable has three possible responses for an editor or reader: thumbs up, thumbs down, or a flat hand tilting from one side to the other. Many submissions fall into flat hand because (a) at least one poem is interesting, (b) the poems are relatively well made, or (c) the editor or reader suspects a first reading may have been too severe and plans to return to the poem or ask someone else's opinion. Acceptances require more than proficiency. (Confession: I had way too many flat-hand undecideds. If I do this again, I'll be much more binary.)

    3. The usual remarks about it being a good idea to have read the magazine are absolutely true. The magazine where I was a guest editor is very appreciative of voice. Any reader of the magazine will see that the poets it publishes all have distinctive voices. While the elements that go into these voices are different, there are common features. For example, they all have control of their diction. They can use conversational language to address important themes. This is the kind of thing that's useful for a poet submitting work to realize, but you can't realize this without reading the magazine. (Another confession: I am uncomfortable with journals that instruct writers to read the magazine before submitting but don't provide free online samples of the writing they like. My friend's magazine is free to read online.)

    4. Don't underestimate the importance of narrative. Nothing engages a reader's attention like a story. Even if the poem is very much a lyric, you need something to wake up the weary editor, and a modicum of story will do that. Otherwise, the reader is left in the realm of

untethered emotion or language, what used to be called "pure poetry." Today, that's not a very exciting place to be.

5. Many of the best poems are conflicted. The problem with political/message poetry is that it is predictable, and unless it is very personal, it will often be a fast thumbs down. It's no help that you and the editor may be in total agreement about the state of society and what to do about it. Yeats pretty much nailed this when he wrote: "Out of the quarrel with others we make rhetoric; out of the quarrel with ourselves we make poetry."

6. Concrete nouns, please! While great poetry can be written full of abstractions, it is rare these days. A poem should convince a reader of its reality. Concrete nouns are the fastest and easiest way to do that.

7. More poets than I'd expect seem to be going along well in a poem and then ruin it by yoking a concrete image to an abstraction with a preposition. Pound used the example—I think from Swinburne—of "dim lands of peace" and declared, "the natural object is always the *adequate* symbol." In other words, if "dim lands" isn't peaceful enough on its own, adding "of peace" to it isn't going to help. Don't they teach this stuff in workshops anymore?

8. Speaking of workshops, there are a lot of poems that have had whatever situated them surgically removed so that readers have no idea what caused the poet to sit down to write it. Is this a workshop thing? It's not clear, but someone somewhere may be teaching writers to cut away at poems to make them mysterious. This may register with certain readers, but to others, it's just a gimmick.

9. Ambiguity for ambiguity's sake is not a great aesthetic principle. We've all read Stevens's lines about how "The poem must resist the intelligence / Almost successfully." First, that's a big "almost." Second, he was

Wallace Stevens; the rest of us aren't. Third, if you don't want to be understood, why publish?

10. The best moment for an editor is when a poem surprises. The poem is by nobody you ever have heard of, and you have no expectations. Then, bang! That poetry bomb goes off in your face. It's what poets want to happen and what editors want to happen. But, that little explosion requires poets to write not just for themselves but to be read by other people, which means you need to have a sense of what you want your reader to experience and a sense of how your work will actually be perceived by others. This is not to say you can please everybody, but if you're not capable of some objectivity about your work, acceptances will be less frequent.

If you're ever offered the chance to guest edit a magazine, I suggest you jump at it. It will change how you view the submission process—at least, it did for me. There's nothing we can do to guarantee that editors will want to publish our poems, but we can write poems that want to be read and that make it reasonably easy for others to read them.

On the Irrational

A close friend died two weeks ago. It was unexpected. He was 49 years old and in excellent health. A blood clot went to his heart, and despite the best efforts of doctors and nurses, he was dead within hours. The family was not religious, but the woman in his life was and organized a "celebration of life" to honor him. I should admit right off that I found it hard to get through this event. A minister had been flown in from another state for the occasion, and he had a particular interest using the event to evangelize. The persons attending were told that the deceased was in heaven, and if they wanted to see their dead friend again, they should accept Jesus as their personal savior. Again right off, I'll acknowledge that I have no expectations in this regard. I had been asked to read a poem at the event and agreed to participate before I was told that it would be a religious event. If I had known, I would not have agreed to read. The poem I had written and read at the outset had as its first line: "I don't believe in God, souls, or ghosts."[1] The minister thanked me "for sharing."

What struck me most at this event was that the participants, including me, found it almost impossible to accept the irrationality of our friend's death. Tomas Tranströmer has a phrase in one of his poems: "the axe blow from inside."[2] I kept thinking about that line. Because

---

[1] I should be clear. I don't go around proselytizing non-belief, and if people can find some kind of consolation in this kind of situation, they should do what they think best. My poem was simply about my own experience of my friend's death and how hard I find it to accept that he is no longer present. The person who asked me to read had read the poem beforehand.

[2] I believe this is from Robert Bly's translation. I am quoting from memory.

most of the attendees were Christians, they had to find providential intent in this unexpected death. I should mention that my friend had been an exceptionally good man who helped many people and sacrificed his own interests continually. So, any idea of transcendent purpose or justice in his death should be dismissed immediately. He did not get what he deserved. Similarly, this was not someone who neglected his physical health. He had not ignored warning signs or failed to get medical treatment. He exercised every day and was in excellent shape. It is not surprising that none of us could understand this sudden violence inflicted on him by his own body.

Despite anthropomorphic religious beliefs and superstitions, human beings are essentially rational. The thousands of decisions we make daily are usually directed toward achieving one goal or another. We praise abilities like intelligence and good judgment because people possessing those abilities are valuable to us as a society, and much of our survival as a species depends on them. I do not know enough about quantum physics to consider the relevance of sub-atomic particles, but in the world I live in, phenomena are considered to happen for reasons. If we did not make this assumption, *a priori*, then the sciences would not exist; they would not produce useful results if this assumption were not correct. This way of approaching the world is so innate to us as humans that we try to apply it beyond understanding *how* things happen. We constantly want to apply reason to *why* things happen. Because we are purposeful creatures, we want to find purpose in everything. We find it hard to accept that the death of someone we love can be meaningless.

The participants at that "celebration of life" were seeking a catharsis that would allow them to go back to their daily lives. A meaningless death reveals a fact of our world as we experience it. Yoga classes, exercise, healthy diets, good medical care, university degrees, satisfying work, and loving family don't stave off such a death. We are contingent beings who have accidents, get sick, and die. The emptiness of this realization is devastating. At least, it is devastating if it occurs not as an abstraction in an essay but as the death of a close friend or family member. When we encounter this emptiness, the *why* of our lives becomes a question without an answer. Anthropomorphic religions generally offer an answer that avoids the question by telling us that the will of the deity is inscrutable. Certain philosophies deny that humans are created with an essence or a purpose and instead place the burden on individuals to create a purpose in their own lives. This too can be an avoidance. To the extent that the grieving person creates by will a purpose out of meaninglessness, the purpose created is at best a functional fiction and at worst something arbitrary and irrational. To substitute *my will* for *God's will* isn't terribly useful as a way to confront the reality revealed by such a death.

I've never thought of myself as a nihilist, but maybe I am. The only response I can see to irrational loss is to acknowledge it, as opposed to finding a purpose in it. This is where we live, and contingency is as much a fact of our lives as gravity or the weather. The question, when it appears, is always singular: "What does it mean *to me* to acknowledge this emptiness? What should *I* do?" I wrote a poem, not because that's any kind of recipe for healing or a preferred response but because it's who I am and how I think and feel. Someone else might legitimately say that I put words together to embody a grief merely as a way to distance myself from it, as though the poem were a small box I could place on some mental shelf. I wouldn't argue with that person. I don't make any claims about my own way of acknowledgment.

The poem may not even have been a particularly good poem. What matters is to find a way to be present in the emptiness created by that death and at the same time to continue.

AGAINST PROMPTS

Prompts are all over social media, and a lot of people seem to like them. The idea is that writers need a little push to get their creative momentum going on its own, so a teacher or facilitator will suggest either a subject to write about or a formal tactic that will hopefully produce a poem or story. Full disclosure: I have lost count of the number of classes and workshops I've taught where I have given assignments and prompts to my students. So, if I see a problem in all this, I am as guilty as anyone of having added to it.

My own misgivings probably started with my reading. I realized one day that the poets I cared about the most don't seem to have sat around responding to prompts. Could a prompt have given us *The Waste Land*? Tennyson's "Tithonus"? Zagajewski's "Going to Lvov"? Szymborska's "Autotomy"? Frost's "Home Burial"? I don't think so. What goes into a piece of writing determines what comes out. Great poems likely originate in great inner conflict, as Yeats put it, our "quarrel with ourselves." They don't rely on suggestions from social media.

It's not that suggestions are inherently bad, however. Remember, it was Rodin who told Rilke he should go to the zoo to study the animals until he could really see them. It that was a prompt, it was a damn good one, and it produced some remarkable poems. Perhaps the difference is that Rodin's advice was to seek out certain kinds of experiences that could lead to poems, not to perform some verbal calisthenics to generate a literary product. If we can deepen our experiences, which we do in all sorts of ways, we may well write better poems or fiction. Of course, different experiences and different writers result in different outcomes. (Admit it, at some point haven't you stood in front of the panther's cage staring for who knows how long and not seeing anything worth writing about? It happens.)

Prompts exist as a shortcut. A writer may suffer from the anxiety caused by a blank page and a mind not ready to do anything about it. Living with that anxiety isn't easy. The assignment is to produce something by the next class. If there's no product by class time, then the student and the teacher will feel they've failed. And, it is the safest of bets that at some point someone, with whatever presumed authority, has declared to them both that writing cannot be taught. Enter the prompt. Even if it results only in fortuitous wordplay, what comes out looks like something that can be brought to class.

I judged a small poetry competition recently, and it occurred to me that a number of the poems I was reading probably originated with a prompt. The tip-off could be an abstraction in the title with a corresponding trope making up the body of the poem. The trope would usually be exhausted in a few lines, but the poem would limp along with a few additional lines of explanation. Another kind of tip-off might be a poem based around a few ambiguous images. I was never sure what those images were actually doing. They seemed to announce a kind of profundity that didn't stand up to examination. Maybe this was my failure as a reader, or maybe it was the kind of poem that happens when the poet is unsure why the poem needs to exist at all. Such poems are highly publishable in certain journals, where the editors favor poems that make the reader work by entering the poem and ascribing meaning to it. This is nonsense, but it's certainly present in the atmosphere. Readers will always ascribe their own meaning to poems regardless of the poem's clarity or lack thereof, but the best poems that resist our understanding are mystical—where the experience is larger than the language that seeks to express it. These do not result from prompts.

The latest development in prompts are the ones that various tech-savvy individuals are giving to web-based artificial intelligence devices in order to receive back literary products they can submit to publishers. Many literary magazines now require potential contributors to certify that they themselves wrote the work in question, not a computer. If this doesn't beg the question, it certainly makes the question obvious: if a computer can respond to a prompt in a way that produces a poem that is difficult to distinguish from a poem by a person that the magazine in question would consider publishing, isn't there something wrong with the literary standards of that magazine? Possibly these journals are so used to receiving ambiguous human responses to prompts purporting to be poems that the editors are worried they've been blinded to the difference between the language of a human voice that is trying to make sense of its world and a conglomeration of vaguely emotive language assembled from the many corners of the internet in response to an AI prompt.

In a few weeks, I'll begin another semester of teaching students to write poems, and I will, hypocritical as it may be, give them assignments, some of which may involve prompts. My reasons are much like those of other instructors. Some of my students will enter the class never having written a poem or a story. Those students need training wheels, and I'm not ashamed to provide them. I teach one day a week in a medium-security prison out in the Everglades. The students enjoy these classes for all sorts of reasons, one of which is that the library, unlike their dormitories, has air conditioning. As the semester progresses, we'll move more and more toward assignments that ask the students to write about the reality of their lives. They are incarcerated, and many live with the knowledge they will never be released. That kind of awareness cannot be counterfeited by artificial intelligence or generated by prompts. We read poems and stories to connect with the experiences of other human beings. We write poems and stories so that readers we don't know will understand the experiences and thoughts that make us who we are. I'm a pragmatist here. If a prompt will enable that process for a little while, I won't refuse it, but if it stands in the way and creates only a clever literary product, then I have no use for it.

Born Too Late?

In the 19th and 20th centuries, we got used to the production of great poems. When *The Waste Land* made its appearance a little over a hundred years ago, readers recognized that something important had happened. They may not all have been pleased, but they recognized the importance. We could say the same for Ginsberg's *Howl*. There are many fine poets writing in the US in the 21st century, but twenty-four years in, there have been no recognizable moments, no poems that challenged us the way Eliot or Ginsberg did—much less Whitman or Dickinson. One way to look at it is to ask yourself "What poem have you read, written in this century by an American, that you felt compelled to memorize?"

This is not a reflection on how a golden age has passed. I merely note that a different kind of writing is being produced now. The culture is more broadly spread, which is to everyone's benefit, and it is certainly less elitist and sexist, again to everyone's benefit. We are not shocked by extreme content anymore, even as we are not shocked by formal innovations. The number of literary magazines and small presses is staggering and constantly in a state of flux. Moreover, most journals are available to us online, which means we don't need to live in New York City or San Francisco to read the most recent poets or to attend exciting readings.

After World War I, Andre Breton wrote: "Beauty will be convulsive, or it will not be at all." What we have learned since, though, is that human beings become dulled to repetition, even to repetition of convulsive beauty. What is convulsive one day is a quiet yawn the next. Kierkegaard's principle of "aesthetic rotation" is more accurate than Breton's manifesto. What thrills us in the morning, bores us in the afternoon.

The virtues of our current poetry are many. The lessons of modernism have been absorbed and are generally remembered. We understand the power of concrete nouns, and we are sensitive to the dictions we use. Grand gestures are blessedly less frequent. At the same time, our poems have a smaller scope of ambition. Poems rarely embrace the big issues these days, and when they attempt to consider history or culture on a large scale, they do so in platitudes or by ironic devices like erasures.

The poetry of our century and country seems to have taken refuge in what Harold Bloom called "*belatedness.*" By that, I mean an almost unconsciously assumed belief that we have come too late to be the great voices of our language. Of course, poets have experienced this feeling all the way back to the Alexandrian Greeks. Milton certainly knew the Bible preceded *Paradise Lost*, but it did not stop him from writing. If we are going to write important poems, much less great ones, we need to take a close look at the symptoms of our malaise.

A few examples:

Beware of the poem that is introduced by "After _____." Notice, please, that no one ever writes "*After Shakespeare's Sonnets*" or "*After Whitman's Leaves of Grass.*" I am not just making a joke. The poems that are being imitated are not the grand products of our civilization; they are usually the small, perhaps virtuous poems of recent poets who may also have been crushed by belatedness. Sometimes, the poem that announces its own belatedness in this way isn't really an imitator of a progenitor poem at all. The poet may be only trying to link the poem to someone more famous. It may become, in effect, a plea for attention.

Beware of clever devices, such as erasures or acrostics or abecedarians, etc. The form is being foregrounded by the poet for a reason. The same thing is true of concrete poetry and poems whose words are spaced oddly around the page. There are many excellent poets who use these formal devices as exercises, a trip to the gym for their compositional muscles. However, if the reason the poem draws attention to the form is a way to make the subject of the poem seem more important or "poetic," then we need to look warily at what is going on.

Beware of poems that originate in workshops. The workshop is a useful venue to teach young poets how to write in certain ways and to allow them to make their mistakes in a supportive atmosphere. Sadly, in the US at least—I don't know about other countries—the workshop and its academic variant, the MFA program, are thought of as ways to generate poetry when the underlying emotion, experience, and thought are not themselves strong enough to do the job unaided. Writing poetry is a lonely business. Poets have traditionally shown their work to trusted friends and relied on each other for reactions. Workshops turned that consultation into a bureaucratic process. There is a further danger, though, that is worse: workshops tend to direct poets into reading mostly, if not only, contemporary work. Having taken and taught my share, I can tell you why. Workshop instructors go in well-justified fear that if their students read work that uses idioms and dictions from other time periods, they will start writing ye-olde-shoppe verse with bad rhymes and contorted syntax. Still, if the students have never read Shakespeare or John Donne, their poems will be the poorer for it, and they will have no larger sense of history.

Beware the cento. There are lines of verse that can make us feel uncomfortably small. This is exactly how we experience belatedness. One response may be to take a whole handful of these lines, put them together, and call them a cento. Yes, Eliot took lines from other poets and used them as tags in *The Waste Land*, but truth be told, they are not his best moments in that poem and often work to show the nervous condition of the speaker. And yes, there were Greek poets who wrote them as homages, but our current examples don't usually suggest that purpose. What is a poet trying to accomplish with a cento? What events, emotions, and thoughts can best be expressed in its form? The cento shows the poet has done some reading, and it's a clever sort of juggling act to put together the disparate lines. However, like other forms cooked in workshop kitchens, it appears mostly utilized to produce a poem that the poet had no real need to write.

Beware of poets who seek to avoid belatedness by not reading. I know some brilliant poets who have never written a poem with a literary reference. If asked, they would probably say they don't want to be part of the elite or don't want to be taken for snobs. They want to write a poetry of ordinary, tv-watching, 9-to-5-working, cook-outs-on-the-weekend human beings. I cannot argue with the quality of their poems. The ones I'm thinking of are really good. That said, it's a big world out there with lots of great poetry that has shaped who we are, whether we know it or not. We don't become better poets by pretending the last few thousand years of poetry don't matter. It's like saying our own DNA doesn't matter. However poets decide to write, they need to read the poets who have come before them. Originality is unlikely to be born from ignorance.

Beware the haiku and its progeny. I have many friends who will likely disown me for the previous sentence. The haiku and the haibun have become ubiquitous American forms. There are several reasons for this, but one stands out: haiku is easy to teach in workshops. "Everybody write a poem with 5 syllables in the first line, 7 in the second, and 5 in the third." What the workshops do not teach is that all poems, especially ones that foreground their form the way American haiku does, need to pass the so-what test. Okay, a creek is running downhill: so what? By all means, read good translations of the great Japanese haiku and tanka poets, and let them shape who you are as a poet and a person, but you should also realize that American imitation of Japanese haiku can sometimes sound just as archaic and boring as the ye-olde-shoppe verse I mentioned above.

Finally, beware of the perfectly planned poem. Such a poem does not make mistakes but has no surprises. The author foregrounds a skill at manipulating language rather than following the poem wherever it leads. You will recognize this kind of poetry because of a certain fatigue that comes over you as you read it. The poet has kept the unconscious on a short lead, and the poem could just as easily have been an essay deduced from a set of logical principles. This type of poem may be especially dangerous because it requires talent, which it then betrays. How to avoid it? Build your poem out of your own conflicted feelings. If you can feel that contradiction in the poem and not be sure of resolution, chances are your poem is alive.

I am not suggesting that we all have a large cup of coffee and start work on writing epics, but we should question why in the 21st century we are writing poems that work so hard to avoid this burden of poetic belatedness. Persons who make a living teaching others to write poems will either dismiss these remarks as the rantings of a modernist who's not dead yet, or they may reply "What would you have us teach?" And, they will have a point. I will even have to admit that I'm a hypocrite in order to respond to them. While I have often taught poetry the same way everyone else has, with formal exercises and assignments based on well-known poems, I know the best way to teach writing is to teach reading. If I have done anything right as a teacher, it's been to give copies of good poems to my students and encourage them to read these poems closely, and if they have learned anything of value in my classes, it has probably come from that reading, not from anything I have said.

I was lucky enough to study with great teachers, who are now the voices of a belatedness that sits on my shoulders as I write. While I remember very few specific comments they made in those many hours of classes, I remember clearly the attention they brought to whatever they read. They read as if each poem were addressed to them personally, and they worked hard to find clues to what the poets had been thinking as they wrote. They believed that if they read closely enough, they'd understand the solutions that other poets had found to the problems they confronted. For them, the past was not a burden, but a storehouse of potential responses. It was there not to teach us how to imitate but how to find our own answers, how to defy belatedness.

What Is a Poem?

Disclaimer: thinking is a disturbing use of time. We start to notice that our everyday lives are built around words we can't define. We can only vaguely describe what we mean when we use them. The more subjective the effects we're describing, the worse it gets. Colors, for example, can be talked about objectively in terms of the visible spectrum of light, but that has very little to do with our perception and response to what we see. We can say something similar for music. And, we are at an utter loss when it comes to using language to understand a creature of language such as poetry.

The common definitions of "poem" are not helpful, to put it kindly. Most talk about beautiful language or language that emphasizes features traditionally associated with poetry, such as meter, rhyme, metaphor, etc. It is easy to think of great poems that avoid most of these features and even easier to think of dull or grotesque linguistic constructions that use meter, metaphor, and rhymes and make us want to crawl under the table. In other words, they may be verse but are certainly not poetry.

Thank you for tolerating my disclaimer. Now that we've acknowledged how entangled and hopeless the whole business is, we can get on to trying to say something useful about what poems are or at least what poems do.

Perhaps the most interesting thing about human beings as a species is that we excel at communication. We're not terribly strong, fast, or furry, but we've done alright for the last three hundred thousand years. (I'm well aware that doesn't mean we'll get through the next hundred years, which is itself a good reason to keep these reflections brief.) Basic informational communication is straightforward: "The waterhole is by the big tree with the twisted trunk." Humans, though, had to do more than that to survive. They had to convince others to help them, to bond with them, and to respond to their desires. It is no accident that one of the largest categories in poetry is love poems of one sort or another. Poetry is a language-tool that human beings developed to communicate complex perceptional and emotional states.

When we encounter a poem, one of the first things we realize is that it presents itself as a poem. It can be recited, read in a book or magazine, even seen on a billboard, but we notice that someone intends us to receive it for something more than informational purposes. It is true that we have didactic poems that range from Hesiod's *Works and Days* to "Thirty days hath September," and these achieve their goal of becoming retained information by use of poetic forms. For the most part though, this is not our sense of what poetry is.

Let's imagine opening a random book at a bookstore or library. On the page is a group of words divided into lines. Perhaps the first word of every line is capitalized, or perhaps not. Perhaps there are no capital letters at all. Perhaps the lines are divided into stanzas or strophes. Just from this, it would be reasonable to assume that the language in front of our eyes is a poem. It is intended as a special kind of communication to us. If it is a lyric poem, the writer wants to give the readers access to a state of mind or emotion. If it's a narrative poem, we anticipate a story meant to engage our emotions and intellect. Or, perhaps we are speaking with a friend and that person turns to us and with a change of vocal tone begins to speak in words that have an observable rhythm or even noticeable rhymes. We know that our friend is trying to communicate something important to us by reciting a poem.

Similarly, the poem may be presented as a part of ritual. All religions use ritualistic language to bring together the practitioners. This ritualistic language announces itself as a communication to a god or to the worshipers, or to some part of the self. Like the lyric or the narrative, we recognize it immediately as poetry.

By announcing themselves as a poem, words, whether written or spoken, explain to us how to receive them. They are words with a purpose, and we are to consider them in light of that purpose. Their significance is not simply informational, even if they contain information. Their goal is not simply to inform us of someone else's state of mind, but to make a state of mind real to us, to make it a part of our own mental and emotional world.

These considerations tell us how we might recognize a poem, but they only begin to tell us what poems are and what they do. If something ordinarily unknowable is presented to me, in this case someone else's state of mind, my immediate question will be "How do I know this is real?" I have no way to verify what Shakespeare was feeling when he wrote a particular sonnet or even to verify what a poet feels who might be sitting in the same room where I'm sitting and reading the poem directly to me. The poem can only convince us of its reality by making connections. If I share none of the experiences that gave rise to the poem and recognize none of the physical details found in the poem, then it is not going to become part of my reality. But, if the poet situates the poem in a way that I recognize, gives me that little bit of backstory that makes me feel at home, I can begin to accept the poem's emotional or intellectual assertions. Further, if the poet uses concrete nouns, brings into the poem the things of the world: the cat, the chair, the pineapple, the wooden table from Peru, then I begin to experience what the poet is experiencing. The poem starts to be real to me, which means a connection has been made, or many connections.

Poems connect us to an experience. Interestingly, we do not have the same experience as the poet. If that were the case, we would lose our own identities in reading the poem, and that's not what happens. We retain our separateness. We may be changed in some way by reading the poem; we may approach our own lives differently, be more aware. But, it's naïve to think that reading poems—and experiencing the connections in that process—will make us better citizens or change for the better political perspectives. If our moral or political views are changed by a poem, chances are that other factors are involved as well. To the extent that poems may change us, they do it subtly. They may make us better able to imagine what it might be like to be someone else or to feel what someone else feels, and they may make us better able to appreciate nuance. Poems often come about because the poet has felt conflicting emotions; the poem allows us to feel that conflict. Yeats, for example, in "Easter 1916" celebrates but doesn't entirely support the Easter rebellion. He tells us how "Too long a sacrifice / Can make a stone of the heart," and questions, "Was it needless death after all? / For England may keep faith / For all that is done and said." The conflict is not resolved. It is embodied in Yeats's verse, in the reciting of the names of the dead and acknowledging the "terrible beauty" of their sacrifice. When we read the poem, we take this unresolved conflict into ourselves, half a world away from Ireland and more than a century away from the writing of the poem. In short, we are connected.

Poetry, then, is a special kind of communication that allows us to connect through the poem to the mind that wrote the poem. It makes use of our perceptions to create a reality that we, as readers, can access. Poems almost inevitably seek to become this reality for the reader.

Sometimes, the words of the poem even go so far as to become mimetic, to suggest in their sound the situation that brings them into being or that is being described. In Christina Rossetti's "Goblin Market," the poet gives us the amazing lines: "Laura stretch'd her gleaming neck / Like a rush-imbedded swan." The sound of the first line, its length of its vowels, its meter, stretch just as Laura stretches to hear the Goblins' voices describing their fruit, while the second line pulls us back into its consonants to create an image in sound of the place where the movement originates. This is consummate poetic skill, but poetry can also seek the real by eschewing such poetic devices in favor of voice and tone. Cavafy in the original Greek certainly uses elegant meters and mixes types of language that are not available in other languages. However, translations of his work into those other languages are usually successful. There is a restrained tone created by diction, subject matter, and point of view that identify Cavafy's poems in whatever language they find themselves and make real the fictional thoughts, actions, and loves of persons dead for two thousand years or alive in twentieth-century Alexandria. Lou Andreas-Salomé wrote to Rilke that in her practice as a psychoanalyst she would read Rilke's poems to her patients because she believed they were helped by his tone. She doesn't say they were helped by his thoughts, observations, or images, but by his tone.

No definition of poetry can be limited to a set of linguistic devices or practices. The poet is always adding, combining, restricting, recombining, even omitting all these. The definition of poetry that we're looking for is not to be found in its features but in its goal: to become as real as possible.

George Franklin practices law in Miami. *Remote Cities* is his third full-length poetry collection with Sheila-Na-Gig Editions, complementing *Noise of the World*, *Traveling for No Good Reason*, and the chapbook *What the Angel Saw, What the Saint Refused.* He has also authored the dual-language collection, *Among the Ruins / Entre las ruinas* (translated by Ximena Gómez and published by Katakana Editores), and a chapbook, *Travels of the Angel of Sorrow* (Blue Cedar Press). He is the co-translator, along with the author, of Ximena Gómez's *Último día / Last Day* and co-author with Gómez of *Conversaciones sobre agua / Conversations About Water* (Katakana Editores).

Sheila-Na-Gig Editions